# Churcn History 101

# Church History 101

## The Highlights of Twenty Centuries

Sinclair B. Ferguson
Joel R. Beeke
Michael A. G. Haykin

**Reformation Heritage Books**
Grand Rapids, Michigan

*Church History 101*
© 2016 by Sinclair B. Ferguson, Joel R. Beeke, and Michael A. G. Haykin

**Reformation Heritage Books**
2965 Leonard St. NE
Grand Rapids, MI 49525
616-977-0889 / Fax 616-285-3246
orders@heritagebooks.org
www.heritagebooks.org

*Printed in the United States of America*
16 17 18 19 20 21/10 9 8 7 6 5 4 3 2 1

Library of Congress Cataloging-in-Publication Data

Names: Ferguson, Sinclair B., author. | Beeke, Joel R., 1952- author. | Haykin, Michael A. G., author.
Title: Church history 101 : the highlights of twenty centuries / Sinclair B. Ferguson, Joel R. Beeke, Michael A.G. Haykin.
Other titles: Church history one oh one | Church history one hundred and one
Description: Grand Rapids, Michigan : Reformation Heritage Books, 2016.
Identifiers: LCCN 2016018360 (print) | LCCN 2016018574 (ebook) | ISBN 9781601784766 (pbk. : alk. paper) | ISBN 9781601784773 (epub)
Subjects: LCSH: Church history.
Classification: LCC BR145.3 .F476 2016 (print) | LCC BR145.3 (ebook) | DDC 270—dc23
LC record available at https://lccn.loc.gov/2016018360

# Contents

# Contents

# Preface

Church history is important for Christians. First, it continues the history of God's faithful dealings with His people found in Holy Scripture and records the ongoing life and work of Christ in our world. Second, we are commanded to "remember all the way which the Lord thy God led thee" (Deut. 8:2) and make it known to our children (Ps. 78:5–6). Third, church history helps to illuminate and clarify what we believe, providing a context for evaluating our beliefs and practices, according to the teaching of the church of all the ages. Fourth, it is a safeguard against error; there are no new heresies, it seems, only old ones masquerading as new. Finally, it gives us mentors and heroes, guides to follow as they followed Christ. In doing so, it promotes spiritual maturation and heartfelt supplication to God to reform and revive His church.

This introduction to church history—a few pages for each century—was first drawn from Sinclair Ferguson's pulpit ministry, then revised by Joel R. Beeke and Michael A. G. Haykin and their respective assistants, Ray Lanning and Coleman Ford. These articles were first published in *The Reformation Heritage KJV Study Bible* in 2014, and are reprinted here under a new title, *Church History 101*. Given the brevity of these articles, the reader will understand that hundreds of important names and events in church history must be omitted. What is recorded will shed light on how Christ has gathered His church, by His Word and Spirit, over the past two thousand years, despite the sins and errors of many theologians and churches. Soli Deo gloria!

## Apostolic Foundations

The first century of church history divides roughly into three periods. In the first, our Lord Jesus, through His ministry, began to fulfill the great promise of Matthew 16:18, "I will build my church." Jesus came into the world to die as the Savior of His people and to build His church. He lived and served, did His mighty works, gave us His teachings and commandments, died, and rose again from the dead that He might fulfill His promise.

The key text for the second third of the first century is Acts 1:8. Jesus told His disciples that they would be His witnesses, "both in Jerusalem, and in all Judaea, and in Samaria, and unto the uttermost part of the earth."

As Acts takes us through the next twenty to thirty years, it records how that promise of Jesus was fulfilled.

First, Christ poured out His Holy Spirit on the apostles and those others gathered in Jerusalem on the Day of Pentecost. In time, they spread throughout the ancient world, preaching the gospel everywhere. In Acts 2, we learn that listening to Peter's sermon were Jews and proselytes from many parts of the ancient world, who took their faith back to their homelands.

Next, Luke reports that Philip the evangelist went down to Samaria. The Samaritans "believed Philip" (Acts 8:12), and Samaria received the Word of God.

Finally, the gospel burst upon the Gentile world through the preaching of Peter (Acts 10–11), and since then, notwithstanding setbacks, has never stopped in its progress to the ends of the earth. We know of Peter's subsequent ministry among the churches in what we now call Turkey (Asia Minor) and farther east in Iraq (Babylon). We know of Paul's ministry in Antioch, then in Turkey and on into Europe. In the last chapter of Acts, Luke records the day Paul came to Rome (Acts 28:16), seat of the far-flung Roman Empire. We know much less about the other apostles, but some of them traveled great distances to preach Christ. Thomas is remembered as the apostle to Persia and India. There is a famous denomination in India called the Mar Toma Church, the St. Thomas Church, which traces its origins back to the preaching of Thomas in the Indian state of Kerala.

Those apostolic believers also began to experience what would become the hallmark of the final third of the first century. As the church of Jesus Christ is built on earth, it faces opposition and often violent persecution. Beginning in the last part of the first century, in the mid-60s, the Emperor Nero turned upon Christians. Rome had burned in a great conflagration. To fend off accusations against himself—for he had sometimes mused out loud about leveling Rome, rebuilding it in marble, and renaming it after himself—Nero blamed the Christians, and a number of believers were martyred in Rome. Some were crucified and some were sewn into the skins of dead animals to be savaged to death by wild dogs.

An early Christian historian named Tertullian wrote in his *Apology*, his defense of the Christian faith, "The blood of the martyrs is the seed of the church," that is, a blessed means whereby Christ plants and grows His church.

# The Church of Martyrs and Confessors

Matthew 16:18 is an important text in the New Testament. The words of Jesus indicate in no uncertain terms that wherever Christ builds His church, there will be powerful opposition to what He is doing, but "the gates of hell shall not prevail against it." Joseph Alexander explains "the gates of hell" as "a strong figure for death, or destruction.... *Gates* has been variously explained to mean the entrance, the defenses, the military force and the judicial power." In other words, Christ promised to build His church in defiance of the enmity and destructive power of death itself.

In the second century of the Christian church, this opposition took two forms. The first was that of *blatant persecution*. There was a human strategy, undoubtedly with a diabolical intent behind it, to destroy the church by destroying its members. Paradoxically, one of the ways in which Jesus Christ has built His church down through the centuries is through the death and testimony of Christian martyrs, as Tertullian observed. In the first century, the Christian church was sheltered to some degree under Judaism, which Rome tolerated as a legal religion. But it became abundantly clear in the early second century that there was a gulf between Jews and Christians. The people of the ancient world spoke about two races of men—Jews and Gentiles. In the second century, they began to speak about three—Jews, Gentiles, and Christians.

Roman law began to accord divine honors to the emperor. Christians, confessing that Jesus is Lord of all, refused to acknowledge the divine lordship of Caesar, and so were guilty of a capital offense. Men and women, boys and girls were slain for their faith in Jesus.

One of the most famous, an old man named Polycarp, declared to the authorities: "I have served Jesus Christ these eighty and six years. He has done me no harm; why should I deny Him now?" The Romans burned him.

A second form of opposition to the building of the church in the second century was *false teaching*. In the second century, the Greco-Roman world was dominated by a dualistic philosophy that regarded the spiritual realm as pure and good, but saw matter as inherently evil. It wasn't long before that philosophy started to distort the message of the Christian gospel in some very basic ways.

First, if spirit is good and matter is bad, then as an eternal and good Spirit, God could not have created the evil material world. It must have been created by some lesser kind of deity, which the false teachers called the demiurge. So the teaching of Scripture began to be eroded: the eternal God was not Maker of heaven and earth. Second, the eternal Son of God could never have become man—that is, taken upon Himself our flesh-and-blood human nature. Therefore, the incarnation was simply the Son presenting only the appearance of humanity. A third implication was denial of the resurrection of the body. Why would God resurrect the body, since, being material, it is inherently bad? At such points, the Christian faith was under attack from this false philosophy.

The church's response was to formulate confessions of the true faith in ways that highlighted that the one true and living God did indeed make heaven and earth and is the Father of our Lord Jesus Christ. These confessions also made it clear that Jesus Christ is both fully God and fully man. The Second Person of the Godhead took upon Himself a full humanity. The martyr Ignatius of Antioch tied together the ways in which the church responded to both persecution and false teaching when he said, "If Christ be not fully human and if he did not really die, why am

I suffering for the gospel and prepared to die for it?"

So in the second century, Christian martyrdom confirmed the truth of the gospel, and the production of the ecumenical creeds began.

# Persecution and Heresy; Origen and Tertullian

How should we respond to persecution and to false teaching? This was the great question facing the third-century church. Theologians who became known as "the Christian apologists" sought to answer this question. The word *apologist* or *apology* relates to 1 Peter 3:15, where Peter says we must be ready to give a "reason" (Greek: *apologia*) for the hope of the gospel that is in us. From the second century, apologists such as Justin Martyr defended the truth of the Christian gospel by expounding Scripture and refuting false accusations regarding the Christian faith. The church also responded to false teaching by quarrying out the true teaching of the Bible.

Two noteworthy figures help us understand how Christ was building the church, yet also show how even the best of Christ's servants stumble and fall. The first of these was Origen. One of the leading thinkers and apologists of the third century, Origen exercised his ministry in the great Egyptian city of Alexandria. At age eighteen, he began to teach in the theological academy of Alexandria. Through his various writings, Origen made important contributions to the understanding of Scripture, not all of which were positive. Being influenced by the Greek philosophical tradition derived from Plato, Origen tended to posit a dichotomy between heavenly things (good) and earthly things (bad). He also believed that there were many layers of meaning in the biblical text, sometimes to the neglect of a plain and literal reading. His method of interpretation would have a profound effect on the way in which Christians would read and understand the Bible.

A second individual who had an enormous influence on the church in the third century was a North African named Tertullian. Born into a pagan family, Tertullian was converted to Christianity later in life. In his ministry, Tertullian wrestled with two important things. First, he confronted the false teaching called *modalism*, an error concerning the persons of the Trinity. Modalists teach that there is one God who has appeared in different ways, or modes—as Father, Son, or Holy Spirit— thus confounding or confusing the persons of the Godhead by denying any real distinction between or among them. This teaching rejects everything Scripture has to say about the communion God enjoys within Himself as Father, Son, and Holy Spirit. Also, it denies the reality of what the Bible has to say about the person and work of our Lord Jesus Christ as the God-man. Tertullian vehemently fought against modalism and, as far as we know, was the first person in church history to use the word *Trinity*.

Tertullian's second problem was the growing moral indifference of professing Christians. Even though people were still being martyred for their faith, Tertullian perceived that unreserved consecration to Jesus Christ was beginning to disappear. He joined a charismatic sect outside the church known as the Montanists, rigorists and ascetics interested in new revelations and prophecies. He felt he had found in the Montanists what he had been looking for in the church at large. Though a zealous defender of the faith, Tertullian tended to divide the Word of God from the Spirit of God, and the Spirit from the Word. He did not grasp the principle so evident in the way Jesus Himself lived His life in obedience to God in the Spirit's power—that to do so, a believer must constantly submit to the teaching God has given in Scripture.

A very important lesson arises from the third-century church: we should never separate the Spirit of God from the Word of God, or the Word of God from our dependence on the Spirit of God. If men of ability and dedication such as Origen and Tertullian found it a tremendous challenge to grasp and apply this principle, we too must take care to study and apply the Scriptures under the Holy Spirit's guidance and illumination.

# The Beginnings of the Christian Empire

The fourth century began with a storm of persecution from without and a time of decay within the visible church. The persecution came from the Roman emperor, Diocletian. He sought to restore stability and peace to the Roman Empire, and was convinced that peace must involve a renewed commitment to the gods of ancient Rome. Diocletian was determined to destroy anything that stood in his way, particularly the Christian church. He sought to destroy places where Christians met, their Scriptures, their leaders, and Christians in general. Diocletian launched an empire-wide persecution. By God's grace, Christians stood firm in the face of such opposition.

At the same time, some Christians were disturbed by an increasing sense of ease and comfort within the church. Standards of Christian living fell as many professed the faith but did not live it. The response of some Christians was to retreat from the temptations of the world and to go into the desert to live solitary lives of prayer, contemplation, and self-denial. These early monastics, despite all their self-discipline, should remind us that Christ has called us not to separate from the world, but to live as witnesses to Christ in the world (1 Cor. 5:10).

Both these influences—an emperor bent on destroying the faith and Christians fed up with a culture not taking the faith seriously enough—had the potential to destroy the witness of the church.

At least three significant events took place in the fourth century. The first was the conversion of the Emperor Constantine. After the famous Battle of Milvian Bridge in 312, he claimed to have seen a vision of the *chi rho* symbol or *labarum*—a monogram using the first two Greek letters in the title *Christ*—and heard a voice say, "In this sign, conquer!" Consequently, when he won the battle, he attributed his victory to Jesus Christ. Immediately he began to relax laws against Christians. Believers were now free to worship Christ without fear of persecution. Christianity became the preferred religion of the empire. Though Constantine did much to help the church, he ultimately hindered it by blurring the distinction between a citizen of this world and a citizen of the world to come.

The second major event was the Council of Nicaea in 325. This council helped clarify what it means for Jesus to be both God and man. An early fourth-century church leader named Arius claimed that Jesus was really a being created by God the Father (Arianism), saying, "There was a time when the Son was not." But the New Testament teaches that Christ is both the Son of God and the Son of Man. If He were not so, He could not reconcile us to God and bring us into God's presence. As a finite creature, His death would not have had infinite power to save us from the infinite guilt of sin against the infinite majesty of God. Fourth-century theologian Athanasius argued for the New Testament view of Christ as the God-man. Thanks to Athanasius, among others, the doctrinal formula produced by the Council of Nicaea, the Nicene Creed, grounded the church in the New Testament view of the person and work of Jesus Christ.

The third great event was the conversion of Augustine of Hippo. A man of great intelligence, his life is documented in his *Confessions*. After a long career in "the pleasures of sin" and as a devotee of a sect known as Manichaeism, Augustine was converted to Christianity when, under deep conviction of sin, he heard a child's voice say, "Take up and read." Seeing an open copy of Paul's Epistles nearby, he took up the book and read the first passage on which his eyes fell (Romans 13:13–14). He felt as if God were speaking directly to him. Augustine did exactly what the text said. He "put on the Lord Jesus Christ" by faith, receiving and resting upon Him for salvation, and was baptized in 387. Augustine's theological legacy can scarcely be exaggerated. Reformed Christians are especially indebted to him; Calvinism is sometimes called Augustinianism. He was a great and influential Christian thinker, yet had it not been for the influence of his mentor, Ambrose; the prayer life of his mother, Monica; and the convicting words of Scripture, we might never have known of him. Such is the grace of God and the power of His Word!

# The City of God and the City of Man

The life of Augustine encompassed two important events in the fifth century. First, barbarian tribes swept into Italy and sacked the city of Rome in 410 and in 455. Rome's reign of power over the nations was broken. One response to this tragedy was to blame the Christians. Augustine responded in his famous book *The City of God*. He argued that from the beginning of history, fallen man has been building his "city" or kingdom over against God. Any kingdom not grounded on the kingdom of God is bound to be transient. The only lasting city or kingdom is the one God is building in Jesus Christ, which Augustine identified with the church. To those who wished to lay blame for the destruction of the great city of Rome at the feet of Christians, he declared: "This is no surprise to us, to see the kingdoms of men rising and the kingdoms of men falling, because our commitment is not to eternal Rome. Our commitment is to Jesus Christ and exclusively to the kingdom He is building." There are two kingdoms, yet only the kingdom of God and His Son, Jesus Christ, will last forever.

Augustine was also involved in the second important event in the life of the church in the fifth century—the Pelagian controversy. The British monk Pelagius, while reading Augustine's famous autobiography, was struck by this prayer: "Grant what Thou commandest, and then command what Thou wilt." In other words, fallen man is utterly dependent upon God's grace for salvation. No one, for example, can practice the self-control or continence God commands unless God gives him grace to do so. These words made Pelagius quite uncomfortable. He believed in a "pull yourself up by your own bootstraps" gospel, in which human beings can amend their lives and be saved by their own efforts.

This great theological controversy engulfed the church. To refute Pelagianism, Augustine had to expound the great Pauline doctrines of grace, such as original sin, fallen man's total depravity and inability to save himself, the efficacy of the atoning death of Christ, and the necessity of faith in Him for salvation. The enormous biblical learning and perseverance of Augustine won the day against Pelagius's teaching in the church.

During this same time, another Briton, Patrick, burdened with concern for the lost and called by God to preach the gospel, demonstrated exemplary missionary zeal. When he was sixteen years old, the family farm was raided by Irish pirates. Patrick was kidnapped, taken to Ireland, and sold into slavery, laboring as a herdsman in County Mayo. During those years as a slave, God opened Patrick's heart, and he yielded his life to Christ. In his early twenties, he escaped and made his way home, where he devoted himself to the life of holiness by becoming a monk.

Feeling called in a vision to return to Ireland, Patrick labored there for the gospel from 432 to 461. His life and work as "the Apostle of the Irish" stand as a testimony to the way God calls certain men and women, even some from obscurity and slavery, to do His will. Through various experiences, God molds their passions and desires, then directs them in some singular way to become Christ's servants. The history of Christianity is adorned with accounts of those who have become signal servants of God from backgrounds of total obscurity.

From these portraits, we learn how important it is to not rely on the kingdom of man. The only lasting kingdom is the kingdom of Jesus Christ. It teaches us that salvation is not by our own accomplishments, but by grace alone through faith in Jesus Christ. It also teaches us that God is at work even in the most adverse circumstances, and can use the most unlikely people to accomplish His saving work among the nations.

## Justinian, Benedict, and the Conversion of the Scots

The sixth century witnessed renewed greatness for the Roman Empire under the reign of Justinian I from 527 to 565. He restored large parts of the empire lost to barbarians in North Africa and Italy. His codification of Roman law became the foundation of legal systems in many European countries. Justinian built many churches, including Holy Wisdom (*Hagia Sophia*) Basilica in Constantinople, considered the greatest church in Christendom. As a defender of orthodoxy, Justinian dealt a blow to paganism by closing the schools of the philosophers in Athens, persecuted Montanists as heretics, and sought to reconcile Monophysites to the orthodox faith.

Monasticism flourished under the leadership of Benedict, whose life mirrors the history of this movement in the life and work of the Western church. Benedict withdrew from life in Rome to live as a hermit, but others came to live with him as disciples. Around 525 Benedict relocated his community to Monte Cassino and wrote his famous "Holy Rule" for the government, worship, and daily work of the monks under his charge. He is remembered as "the patriarch of Monasticism."

We turn now to Scotland in the sixth century. By the standards of continental Europe, Scotland was regarded as a barbaric and uncivilized land. The area was controlled by four warring tribes. First there were the Picts, or the "painted ones," as the Romans called them; they inhabited large tracts of Scotland, living largely north of the River Forth. Then there were the Angles, who lived between the River Forth and the River Humber. Also, there were in the west the Britons, making Dumbarton their central place of activity and ruling over the region of Strathclyde. Finally there were the Scots, who originally came from Ireland, invading Scotland at the beginning of the sixth century. The country was characterized by total paganism, and the Druids acted as the pagan priests of the land. The country was desperately in need of the power of the gospel. It soon came to Scotland through the tireless work of two individuals.

One of them was Ninian. Most scholars believe he lived in the sixth century and labored in southwest Scotland in the area of Whithorn. Living in obscurity, Ninian gathered a small number of men around him and created a monastic community. By replicating this little community, he sought to evangelize the Picts, accomplishing his task with considerable success.

This pattern of planting Christians where no Christian witness existed was pioneered by Ninian and popularized by Columba, an Irish monastic from the region of Donegal. Columba came to the little island of Iona off the west coast of Scotland, and there he established a small monastery. This group devoted themselves to prayer, to the study of Scripture, and to providing for one another, and eventually grew into a community of well over a hundred. From Iona, Columba began his challenging task of evangelizing the rest of Scotland. Cell groups of disciples were planted throughout different parts of the country, waging spiritual warfare with paganism and demonstrating what it meant to live out the gospel in community.

By the witness of Ninian, Columba, and other, lesser known individuals, many of the diverse peoples of Scotland came to know Jesus Christ. Two things stand out about these men. To historians, Ninian is an obscure figure with little to no background or claim to fame. Perhaps the only reason why the name of Ninian endures in Scotland is his ministry to evangelize the Picts. Faithful service is often unnoticed by men but it never remains unnoticed by God. Another lesson we learn from both Ninian and Columba is that the power of the gospel is demonstrated not only through preaching and teaching, but through the transformed Christian community. In the pattern of the New Testament, cell groups went out to be the local church in order to demonstrate Christ's grace to transform lives. Though there are various theological points where Ninian and Columba strayed from Scripture, many churches and denominations today can learn from them that grace-filled interaction between Christians will draw unbelievers to see that there is something supernaturally wonderful about Jesus Christ's kingdom.

# Gregory the Great and the Rise of Islam

Two figures are particularly significant for the history of the church in the seventh century. The first figure is Gregory the Great. The son of a wealthy and influential Italian family, Gregory decided to follow a monastic path rather than the family tradition of public service. He eventually became the bishop of Rome. Gregory was a man of considerable organizational ability and significant vision. His times were constantly filled with turmoil, as ownership or control of Rome often went to the highest bidder or the barbarian group with the most might. Gregory sought to bring the entire world into the faith by sending bands of monks and evangelists to baptize and place

the name of Christ over the nations. Rulers
and kings were successfully won to the church.
Nations at large were baptized into the faith.
The church, so it seemed, was beginning to
reign not only spiritually but also with earthly
powers among the nations. But the Christian
faith that was produced was like "the form of
godliness" without the power of it (2 Tim. 3:5).
Gregory's vision produced a kind of nominal
Christianity with which the church continues
to struggle to this day.

The other person who was infamously
significant was Mohammed. Born in the late
sixth century, Mohammed suffered from various strange illnesses, including what may have
been epilepsy. He was untutored, uneducated,
and possibly even illiterate. When he was a
young man, he married a woman some fifteen
years older than himself, the widow of a rich
merchant, and became a trader. As he traded,
he met Jews and Christians, and began to
listen to what they professed to believe. The
Christians he met were likely unorthodox or

even gnostic groups—those who professed faith in Christ, but whose theology and practice deviated at key points from the faith of the historic church.

When he was older, Mohammed claimed to have several visions. The first of those visions was of the archangel Gabriel, who Mohammed believed was calling him to be the prophet of God. Responding to that vision, he began to teach what would become the foundational tenets of Islam. At first, in Mecca, he found very little response. Then, in 622, he fled to Medina, where he began to gather large numbers of followers. Within ten years, he had gathered as many as fifty thousand followers. By the turn of the century, within eighty years of Mohammed's original vision, Islam began to sweep through the Middle East. It saw success in North Africa, often through sheer brutality. But its advance ground to a halt in Spain. In the end, those who claimed to follow Allah and his prophet Mohammad conquered nearly half of the Roman

Empire. The historic Christian communities of the Near East and North Africa were either destroyed or reduced to the status of despised and oppressed minorities.

Mohammed denied the deity of Christ and denied that Christ Himself died on the cross. He taught that salvation does not come through someone else's work on a person's behalf, but through a self-willed submission to Allah. In Islam, salvation knows nothing of God's grace in Christ or of the substitutionary atonement, of Christ bearing the sins of man and offering them assurance of salvation. Islam was and remains a manmade religion because it can never offer what only God can offer in and through Jesus Christ—that is, mercy, grace, and salvation for fallen, sinful human beings.

So what was the church doing when Islam was on the rise? One of the most famous gatherings of churchmen that took place in the last third of the seventh century was the Synod of Whitby, which met in England in 684. It was a gathering of bishops wrestling with the "significant" issues of their time: the shape of the tonsure worn by priests and monks, and the date of Easter. This historical example shows how sometimes the church can completely forget its mission. While there is a time and season for everything, the church must not forget what matters most: it must remain clear and steadfast on the Great Commission, not just claiming land and nations for earthly gain, but proclaiming the gospel to a lost and dying world.

# The Iconoclastic Controversy

Students of church history need to understand the two dominant languages and traditions present within the ancient church. In the Western church, the church that tended to center around Rome, the primary language for writing and worship was Latin. In the East, the primary language of the church was Greek. These languages symbolize the different ways in which these two church traditions developed. As the Roman Empire disintegrated, these traditions lost contact with each other and developed in separate ways.

An eighth-century controversy demonstrating the differences between these traditions was the disagreement over the use of

icons in the worship of God. Icons are depic-
tions of Jesus, Mary, the saints, and sometimes
the persons of the Trinity, among others, and
came to have particular significance in the
Eastern church. Those in favor of icons argued
that pictures were necessary as "books to
the laity," that is, for communicating biblical
truth to the illiterate and uneducated, and for
helping to focus worship in the proper direction. The object of worship was not the image
or icon, but the person, divine or human, it
represented.

However, many began to think that icons
were channels through which Christ was
speaking to them and through which God
was blessing them. Christians in the East
would kneel before them, perhaps would kiss
them as holy objects, and on occasion would
light candles or burn incense before them as
an expression of their desire that through the
intercession of the person depicted by the icon,
the heavenly Father would hear their prayers.

These practices caused a great division in the eighth-century church between *iconodules* (literally, "servants of icons") and *iconoclasts* (literally, "breakers of icons"). The controversy came to a climax in 787 at the Second Council of Nicaea. The church eventually acceded to the use of icons, insisting they not be worshiped but used only for instruction and veneration, that is, only for giving honor to the one depicted. Throughout the centuries, however, the line often became blurred as images were accorded an ever more important place in public worship and private devotion. By contrast, the making of such images, as well as worshiping or serving them, was forbidden by God in the second commandment. Yet men always attempt to be wiser than God, it seems.

Reflecting on the iconoclastic controversy, Protestants should remember the biblical "images" or "visual aids" we have been given to help us understand the gospel. The New Testament witness affords the church two—baptism and the Lord's Supper. Throughout the New

Testament, Christians are encouraged to continually reflect on the significance of these two sacraments, "wherein, by sensible signs, Christ and the benefits of the New Covenant are represented, sealed, and applied to believers" (Westminster Shorter Catechism, Q. 92). Although we must be justly critical of the use of icons in the church, we also ought to be critical of ourselves for paying so little attention to the "sensible signs" that Jesus has given to us.

Though synods and councils may be preoccupied with internal disputes, in every century of the church there are those whose eyes are turned outward to see the great need of the world. Two such people from the eighth century exemplify this outward gaze. The first is Boniface, remembered as "the Apostle of the Germans." Born at the end of the seventh century in Crediton, Devon, he gave himself to the service of Christ and the church, spending his life evangelizing various parts of the world, including Frisia, Thuringia, and Bavaria. Boniface often found himself in the midst of pagan cultures, yet he stood against them with the power of the gospel. He was eventually martyred for Christ in the year 754.

The other example from the eighth century is Olopan or Alopan. The Sigan-Fu stone, discovered in northwest China in the early seventeenth century by Roman Catholic missionaries, recorded the advent of Christianity in China from 150 years prior to the time of its inscription, circa 780. It recounted the work of Olopan, an Assyrian missionary who had come from Syria to China to preach the gospel. By the eighth century, Chinese emperors were persecuting Christians and extinguishing the flame of the gospel in China. To their astonishment, the missionaries who discovered the Sigan-Fu stone one thousand years later learned what people in the seventh and eighth centuries had been willing to do and to sacrifice for Jesus Christ in China.

# Struggle for Power in the Church; Ratramnus and Gottschalk

One of the great tension points of the ninth century was a clause in the Nicene Creed. The inclusion of this clause in the text of the creed would eventually lead to a great division between the Western church and the churches of the East.

In some ways, it was a theological difference, a difference in understanding the relationship of the Spirit to the Father and Son. But it was also part of a power struggle in the worldwide visible church and between two of its leaders: the pope, or bishop of Rome, Nicholas, a man of considerable organizational skills, and the theologian and preacher Photios, the patriarch of Constantinople. In other words,

the dispute over the creed became a battle-
ground in the long campaign to establish the
supremacy of the pope over all Christendom.

In the midst of this controversy, Pope
Nicholas appealed to what scholars refer to as
the Pseudo-Isidorean Decretals. These doc-
uments gave the bishop of Rome supreme
authority over the ecumenical or worldwide
church. They were certainly not written by
Isidore of Seville, but were fabricated by an
unknown source at a much later period. Patriarch Photios objected to these assertions, as
did all the other patriarchs and bishops of the
Eastern churches.

Despite this conflict over the claims of
the papacy, individual figures were arising in
the church with a great zeal to see Christ's
kingdom extended. In the mid-ninth century,
two brothers from Thessalonica, Cyril and
Methodius, set out to spread the gospel to
the region that would later become Russia.
Today they are often called "the Apostles of
the Slavs." They devised the Cyrillic alphabet

in order to translate the Scriptures and the church's liturgy into Slavonic, as essential tools for preaching Christ to the Slavic nations of Eastern Europe. They were able to evangelize the entire region around the Black Sea. The presence of Christian churches in many of these places today can be traced back to their evangelistic work.

Another significant theologian from the ninth century worth mentioning is Ratramnus of Corbie, who wrote in opposition to his fellow monastic Paschasius Radbertus, who propounded transubstantiation, the notion that the consecration of the communion bread and wine changed these earthly elements into the flesh and blood of Christ. Ratramnus also defended predestination, though he was not as zealous in this as was Gottschalk.

Born in Saxony, Gottschalk was given over by his parents to be a servant in the church. Gottschalk became fascinated by Augustine's writings. Augustine had emphasized that we are not just spiritually sick, but are, as Paul says in Ephesians 2, dead in trespasses and sins. Gottschalk began to reflect on God's grace in electing some to salvation. But he also observed that many leaders in the church were teaching salvation by works righteousness. Gottschalk argued that we need to grasp that salvation, which we receive through faith, is a gift that God planned to bestow upon us before we were born. Like Augustine before him, Gottschalk left no place for any individual contribution in gaining righteousness before God. Our faith and works are merely reflections of the salvation we have received, not a contributing factor to it.

Though he preached salvation by grace alone, Gottschalk sometimes presented his case in an unwise manner. He was passionate about double predestination, that is, the doctrine that God has assigned some to eternal life as well as many to eternal punishment. His passionate preaching led eventually to his condemnation as a heretic. He was deposed from his ministry and imprisoned for twenty years.

Gottschalk challenged the condemnation and requested that he be allowed to undergo a trial by ordeal to reveal whether or not he was truly a heretic. He strongly believed he would be vindicated as a preacher of biblical truth.

Though Gottschalk was not as temperate as he should have been, he was right about our contribution to salvation. The moment we begin to think that we contribute something to our salvation, it ceases to be the salvation of grace taught in the New Testament. The church should honor Gottschalk's memory despite his human frailties. We should also continue to educate ourselves about missionaries such as Cyril and Methodius, and remember that the quest for power and recognition, demonstrated by Pope Nicholas, ultimately detracts from the mission and witness of the church.

# "The Dark Ages"

We sometimes say that history repeats itself. At the end of the first millennium, the situation of the church was much the same as we face today. In the tenth century, the church was in decline theologically though not culturally and politically. We call this period "the Dark Ages," and in some ways, the description is accurate. Once-strong empires and kingdoms were beginning to crumble. The balance of power was shifting toward the church and territorial boundaries were shifting as well.

Another similarity is the nominal Christianity of the tenth century. Part of this nominalism resulted from the struggle for power and influence outside the church, which led to neglect of cultivating faith on the inside. The power gains of the church tended to corrupt the church and her leaders. Educational standards fell, and many of those who ministered God's Word were altogether ignorant of it. An ignorant ministry could not arrest the inherent decay in society with the power of the gospel. New political powers from the north (the Vikings or Norsemen) and the south and east (Muslims) swept in, challenging the worldly power of the church. The church responded with little to no spiritual direction for its members.

One exception came from a group of monastics at Cluny in eastern France. These Benedictine monks, seeing the spiritual decline all around, devoted themselves to the study of Scripture, the worship of God, simplicity of Christian living, and various other spiritual disciplines. They recognized that by and large, the members of the church had lost their zeal to know the Lord and live in devotion to Him. Leaders of the church had become worldly-minded and disinterested in spiritual matters. The Cluniac reform began as one of the more spiritual efforts of the Middle Ages, but the movement would itself suffer decay and yield to temptations to worldliness, requiring yet another reform in the following centuries.

In the last years of the tenth century, Christianity extended its reach into Russia with the baptism of Prince Vladimir and his twelve sons at Kiev in 988. Vladimir embraced Christianity upon receiving the reports of envoys sent to Constantinople. They gave a positive account of the faith and worship of that great city, and were impressed by the splendor of Justinian's Holy Wisdom Basilica. The pioneering work of Cyril and Methodius among the southern Slavs had prepared the way by furnishing a liturgy and a body of Christian literature in Slavonic. Most of the people of Kiev followed their prince's example, and thousands were baptized in the Dnieper River. From such beginnings sprang the Russian Orthodox Church.

The close of the first millennium of the Christian era found the church in a position of cultural dominance, at least within the boundaries of the Roman Empire. The church also had had no small measure of success in surviving barbarian invasions and converting the invaders.

As the empire was divided and began to retreat in the face of the invading barbarians, the church was likewise divided, East and West. The Eastern church lived under the protection of the Roman emperors, who now reigned in Constantinople. She enjoyed imperial patronage, but also suffered much from imperial interference in her affairs. The Western church had to stand alone, filling the vacuum left behind as the seat of empire shifted to the East. The popes of Rome were in a position to take power into their own hands, and they did so, with no one to call them to account. Large parts of Italy were ruled by the popes, who owned huge tracts of land, using the revenues of those lands to fund their campaigns to dominate both the world-wide church and the rulers of the many kingdoms and principalities under their sway.

Today's world is not much different from that of the tenth century. The church continues to be confronted with paganism, as well as with temptations to worldly success. While some denounce the tenth century as "the Dark Ages," we must recognize that our contemporary society demonstrates a moral and spiritual darkness, and the church is challenged to respond with the light of the gospel. Sometimes the church stands by and lets her witness be muted by worldly concerns. Rather, the church should perpetually increase in the knowledge of God's Word, be strengthened by the worship of God, and give itself to the simplicities of day-by-day devotion to Jesus Christ. By living for Christ and proclaiming the gospel, we can shine a much-needed light in the darkness.

# The Great Schism; Anselm of Canterbury

The eleventh century still found the church in a dark place, though glimmers of light continued to shine through. One of its darkest events, usually referred to as the Great Schism, took place in 1054. The de facto division between the Latin-speaking Western church and the Greek-speaking churches of the East was made absolute and irreconcilable. The pope of Rome and the patriarch of Constantinople excommunicated each other, and the bodies of churches under the authority of each were arrayed against each other as hostile camps. The unity of the visible church was broken, and remains broken down to our time.

The disagreement centered on the addition of the *filioque* (that is, "and from the Son') clause to the Nicene Creed. In the fifth century, Western scholars, under the influence of Augustine, had begun to look afresh at the Scriptures regarding the relationship of the Spirit to the Father and the Son. They came to the conclusion that the Scriptures teach that the Holy Spirit proceeds not only from the Father, but also from the Son. Therefore, from the fifth century onward, the Western Church had added the *filioque* clause to the relevant article of the Nicene Creed, giving it the form in which it has come down to us today: "I believe in the Holy Ghost, the Lord and Giver of life; who proceedeth from the Father and the Son."

The Eastern churches took issue and appealed to the original formulation of the Council of Nicaea, arguing that the Latin-speaking Western church did not have authority to alter a formula adopted by an ecumenical council. But behind this concern was the objection of the Eastern churches to the Western claim that the pope was the supreme bishop of the worldwide church and the "vicar" or representative of Jesus Christ on earth.

One glimmer of light during this dark time was Anselm of Canterbury, a gifted intellectual and a man of considerable spiritual and moral courage. Anselm promoted his famous ontological argument for the existence of God and served the church by providing thoughtful theological argumentation and philosophical analysis regarding the existence and nature of God.

Anselm's *Cur Deus Homo*, or *Why Did God Become Man?* plumbed the depths of the atonement of Jesus Christ and the purposes of God that stood behind it. He argued that God's justice requires Him to punish sins committed against His infinite majesty with everlasting punishment of the sinner, in body and soul. As sinners, our only hope is to find a mediator and deliverer who is very man and perfectly righteous, and therefore able to satisfy for our sins; but also very God, more powerful than all creatures, and therefore able to sustain the burden of God's wrath and obtain righteousness and eternal life for us. Our Lord Jesus Christ, who is "very God and very man," is the Savior God has provided for us.

During this time, many within the church recognized the corruption bred by the close relationship between church and state. From the time of Constantine, kings had claimed the right to appoint bishops for the churches under their rule, and they naturally chose men who favored their policies and helped them curry favor with the people. Beginning in the eleventh century, a series of popes began to challenge the authority of monarchs in this practice. The conflict became known as the Investiture Controversy, so named because the kings who appointed the bishops invested them with titles, possessions, and other temporal rights, as well as the symbols of their office, including a gold staff, or crosier, and a gold ring. Pope Gregory VII responded by asserting the power of the church to elect bishops and translate them (move them from one see to another). The pope also asserted his power over the Holy Roman emperor, citing the coronation of Charlemagne in the ninth century as a precedent. The conflict would continue into the twelfth century, finally ending with the pope securing most of the power for which he and his predecessors had contended.

This result encouraged the popes to involve themselves more and more in secular affairs and to exercise an ever-greater measure of political and even military might, at ever greater financial cost to the church. The popes became the first geo-politicians, and burdened themselves with the perpetual need to raise funds by any means, fair or foul. Worldly-minded popes had little concern for the spiritual well-being of the church, and little or no interest in her true calling and mission in the world.

# The Crusades, Abelard, Lombard, and the Waldenses

As the eleventh century gave place to the twelfth, the church began to reap the bitter fruits of the Great Schism of 1054. Signs of division continued to appear across the landscape. One consequence of this division was the unfortunate series of Christian military campaigns known as the Crusades. These expeditions, incited by the pope and backed by various kingdoms of the West, sought to combat the threat of Islam and retake Jerusalem and the "Holy Land" of Palestine.

The First Crusade began in the last few years of the eleventh century, and subsequent crusades were launched throughout the twelfth century. The Second Crusade (1145–1149) was incited by the famous monk Bernard of Clairvaux, who declared: "Pagans must not be slain if they may by other means be prevented from oppressing the faithful. However, it is better they should be put to death than that the rod of the wicked should rest on the lot of the righteous. The righteous fear no sin in killing the enemy of Christ. Christ's soldier can securely kill and more safely die. When he dies, it profits him; when he slays, it profits Christ." Rather than relying on the spiritual weapons of faith, love, prayer, evangelism, and good works, the church looked to political, military, and financial might to answer the threat of Islam.

It was thought that the only language the Islamic forces would understand was the language they themselves spoke—the language of violence. The Crusaders failed to understand that Christ enjoins His people to speak a different language. Our means and ends should be those of Jesus. Ours should be a language of humility and love in the name of Christ, not violence, slaughter, and retribution.

Regrettably, the Crusaders did not distinguish Eastern Christians and Jews from their Muslim overlords, and so they, too, were assailed with fire and sword. In the end, the Crusades failed to achieve their announced objectives. They are a dark stain on the Christian church.

One noteworthy figure from the twelfth century was Peter Abelard, perhaps more famous for his love affair with Heloise than for his theology. He was, however, one of the most influential theologians of his day. He taught a substantially different view of the atonement than Anselm, asserting that man is saved by the extraordinary demonstration of God's love in Jesus Christ. Such a demonstration should overwhelm us and cause us to respond to God in faith. But Abelard failed to see that what is amazing about the love of God is the fact that "while we were yet sinners, Christ died for us" (Rom. 5:8). Scripture connects love and propitiation: "Herein is love, not that we loved God, but that he loved us, and sent his Son to be the propitiation for our sins" (1 John 4:10). If Christ's death is not a satisfaction for sin, then it is reduced to an extravagant gesture on God's part.

Also worthy of mention is Peter Lombard, author of *The Sentences,* a compilation of quotations from church fathers on various facets of theology. From the twelfth to the sixteenth centuries, students of theology were often required to write an exposition and commentary on Lombard's *Sentences.* Lombard's method was characteristic of the times, when theological discussion and debate consisted largely of appeals to decrees of councils, opinions of ancient writers, and doctrines of men.

Noteworthy in twelfth-century France was the origin of the Waldenses and the Waldensian movement, founded by Peter Waldo, who preached in Lyons (1170–1176) and gathered followers known as "poor men" because they stressed poverty and simplicity of life. The Waldenses objected to many of the errors and corrupt practices of the Western church later targeted by the Reformers in the sixteenth century. They soon spread beyond France after being placed under a papal ban in 1184. They endured many centuries of bitter persecution, but have continued down to our time as part of the evangelical family of churches.

Many lessons can be learned from this period. One prime lesson is that when the agenda of the world becomes the agenda of the church, the church's true calling is cast aside. Although the church of the twelfth century fell into this error, its light was not extinguished. God did not leave Himself without a witness. Christ did not forsake His church, even in the darkest of ages. Ultimately, we need to remind ourselves to bow at the feet of Jesus, who is our teacher, follow His agenda, and live a gospel-centered lifestyle as witnesses to the world.

# Francis of Assisi and Thomas Aquinas

A significant symbol of the spiritual condition of the Christian church at the end of the twelfth century is the capture of Jerusalem by Saladin in 1187. Then too, the Crusades of the eleventh and twelfth centuries—which continued throughout most of the thirteenth century as well—underline for Christians today just how far the church had strayed from Christ's gospel. The church preached bloodshed as a way of defending relics and sacred places of the Christian faith. To be spiritual was to fight. The transformative teaching of the gospel had fallen into decay.

However, there were groups and individuals in the thirteenth century who were concerned with refocusing the church on the teaching of Christ and the apostles. Consequently, the thirteenth century became known for its Western religious orders.

The Roman Catholics continued to ascribe an important role to the monastic orders of the Benedictines, Cistercians, and Premonstratensians. Many of the Mendicant Orders, which focused primarily on preaching, pastoral ministry, and poverty, were founded in this century. The four Mendicant Orders recognized by the Second Council of Lyon are the Order of Preachers (Dominicans), founded in 1215 by Dominic de Guzman; the Hermits of St. Augustine (Augustinians), founded in 1256 by communities that followed the Rule of St. Augustine; the Order of Mount Carmel (Carmelites), which came to Europe in the thirteenth century; and the Friars Minor (Franciscans), founded in 1209 by Francis of Assisi.

Francis was one of the most influential people among those who wanted to purge the

church of the power of the sword. He was born
just about the time of the fall of Jerusalem.
Francis began his adult life as a soldier, but
when he heard a sermon from Matthew 10 that
explained how Jesus sent out His disciples to
proclaim the kingdom without dependence on
earthly goods, he was radically transformed.
He gave himself to a life of simplicity and a
great concern for preaching repentance as the
way into the kingdom of the Lord Jesus Christ.
Though he imbibed many of the serious theological errors of Roman Catholicism, Francis
sought to point the church back to a simplicity
of lifestyle.

Another important figure arose in the
thirteenth century—Thomas Aquinas, a
Dominican who is often regarded as one of the
church's great scholastic thinkers. Scholasticism had its origins in attempts to reconcile the
philosophy of ancient classical philosophers
with medieval Christian theology. Though
it never became a philosophy or theology in
itself, it played an important role as a tool

and method for learning that underscores the importance of dialectical reasoning. One of scholasticism's main purposes was to answer questions and resolve apparent contradictions.

Born in 1224, Thomas was by nature quiet and shy. Based on these traits and his substantial physical proportions, others referred to him as "the dumb ox." Soon after he entered a Dominican monastery, Thomas's theological acumen became evident. Thomas's mentor, Albertus Magnus, recognizing his intellectual potential, scolded the other monks for taunting him and famously stated, "This dumb ox will fill the world with his bellowing." Albertus Magnus was himself an accomplished philosopher and theologian, and provided considerable guidance to Thomas.

Aquinas produced two major works, *Summa Contra Gentiles* and his *Summa Theologica*. The first was a defense of the Christian faith against paganism. He was concerned to use his powerful intellect to help Christians spread the gospel where it was not known.

*Summa Theologica,* or *The Sum of Theology,* was a detailed analysis of the content of the Christian faith. One of Thomas's leading principles was that philosophy should be employed as the handmaiden of theology; that is, the tools of philosophy should be put to work in the exposition and defense of theological truth.

Aquinas is noteworthy for his defense of the literal sense of Scripture as the primary and authoritative sense. But ultimately, Thomas accepted the authority of the church. He was content to expound and defend the received teachings and practices of the church, whether they accorded with Scripture or not. One critic said that Thomas's system of doctrine and ethics was "merely an echo of the doctrinal teaching of the church." As able as Thomas was in many respects and as sincere as many of the monks no doubt were, later reformers would come to see the theological problems associated with Thomas's Semi-Pelagianism and the practical problems of the Western religious orders.

# The Church's Babylonian Captivity and John Wycliffe

Sadly, the church hierarchy continued to pursue worldly power in the fourteenth century. The popes persisted in their bid for dominance in political affairs. While the church must be in the world, working to bring about change and draw people to Christ, we are never to be of the world. The church should not thirst for power or seek to assert its authority through political means. In the fourteenth century, the ambitions of popes and kings embroiled the church in ecclesiastical civil war.

Pope Boniface VIII involved himself in numerous political dealings to give the papacy more autonomy and authority. On the other hand, Philip IV, king of France from 1285 to

1314, sought to take advantage of family ties to Italian nobles to enhance his power over the French clergy. Measures by Boniface to secure the church against political interference enflamed the opposition of Philip and his allies.

Boniface died in 1303. His successor, Benedict XI, was not long on the papal throne when he, too, died. Rumors circulated that he had been poisoned. Clement V, Benedict's successor, was a French cleric elected with the help of French funds, a pope who would certainly be more sympathetic to Philip IV's exercise of authority over the French church. Soon after, Clement decided to relocate the papacy from Rome to Avignon in France. The French monarchs effectively owned the pope and controlled the church for seventy years. This was certainly a case in which the mission of the church was turned upside down to serve worldly interests.

The Italian poet Petrarch called this subversion of the papacy the "Babylonish captivity of the church," alluding to the Babylonian exile of the Jews in the sixth century BC. He also decried Avignon as the immoral "sewer of the world." Dante Alighieri, author of *The Divine Comedy*, placed Pope Boniface VIII in the Eighth Circle of Hell, among the simoniacs (those who practiced simony, that is, who sold offices of the church to the highest bidder).

Catherine of Sienna, a notable Catholic mystic and nun, appealed to Pope Gregory XI in 1376 regarding the "sins" of Avignon. Based on her appeal, Gregory returned to Rome in order to restore the papacy there, but he died a year later. Conflict regarding the election of his successor in Rome led to the Papal Schism of the early fifteenth century. When Urban VI was chosen to succeed Gregory, disaffected clerics withdrew to Avignon and elected Clement VII. Rival popes reigned in Rome and at Avignon from 1378 to 1429.

A noteworthy luminary in this period was John Wycliffe. One of his teachers, Thomas Bradwardine, championed orthodoxy against

Pelagianism and came as close as any fore-runner of the Reformation to embracing the doctrine of justification by faith alone. An outstanding scholar, Wycliffe was the master of Balliol College in Oxford. He became concerned about the low spiritual state of the visible church. His concern led him back to the basic principle that Holy Scripture should be the church's rule of faith and practice.

In 1382, Wycliffe translated the Latin Bible into the English of his day so that the people might have the Word of God in their own language. His translation has influenced all succeeding English versions of the Bible. His followers, the Lollards, stressed the primacy of preaching, denied transubstantiation, questioned the papacy, and influenced later men and movements, including John Huss and the Reformation. Often cited to answer charges in church courts, Wycliffe refused to be silenced and went on with his work. After his death, the Council of Constance excommunicated him posthumously in 1415 and had his remains disinterred, burned, and cast into a river.

From Wycliffe's life, we learn the importance of getting the Word of God into the hands of the people. Despite the fact that the church's hierarchy was beset with ambitions for earthy power, some were focused on helping people know God's Word and be transformed by the gospel. Because of this conviction, Wycliffe is often referred to as "the morning star of the Reformation." Today we must see that the church exists to bring light to the world, and we must be willing to separate earthly power and gain from the mission of the church. The church accomplishes her mission by the power of the Holy Spirit, not by the might of kings or political leaders.

# The Renaissance, Huss, Savonarola, and Groote

The fifteenth century was the age of the European Renaissance, an extraordinary rebirth in social life, the arts, and intellectual activity under the banner *ad fontes* ("back to the sources" or "to the fountains"). As part of a general quest to recover the lost riches of classical antiquity, scholars began to go behind the received Latin translation of the Scriptures to study the original Hebrew and Greek texts, to discover more accurately what the New Testament itself said about the Christian faith. Two men of the fifteenth century exemplify this renewed enthusiasm for searching the Scriptures.

The first was Jan Huss. Born in 1373, Huss came from Bohemia, today's Czech Republic. As a young man, he became rector at the University of Prague. He began to study the writings of men who were going back to Scripture, especially those of John Wycliffe. Huss soon realized that the teaching of the New Testament was at odds with the teachings of the church of his day. He asked himself how there could be such a dramatic difference between the faith proclaimed in the Scriptures and the faith demonstrated in the church. When he began to preach about these concerns, he met with considerable opposition. He was excommunicated and urged to repudiate his writings while on trial. His answer was that if his opponents could show him from the New Testament where he had gone wrong in his writings, he would repudiate them immediately. His challenge was received with indignation, but went unanswered. Huss was burned at the stake as a supposed enemy of the faith.

The second man was Girolamo Savonarola, a Dominican monk in Florence, Italy. Savonarola labored in his preaching until he had gained a reputation as a profound expositor of Scripture. People daily crowded the cathedral in Florence to listen to his preaching. Those listening were often convicted by the power of the gospel. Transformation soon followed, demonstrating the power of the preached Word.

Savonarola's success as a preacher, however, did not escape the eye of the ecclesiastical authorities. To silence Savonarola, the pope offered him promotion to high office, but he declined. He soon found himself rejected at every turn. Local leaders stirred up resistance against him. He was arrested, imprisoned, and tortured by the Inquisition. Like Huss before him, Savonarola was burned to death for the biblical message that he refused to recant.

Mention also should be made of Gerard Groote. In the Netherlands in the late fourteenth century, Groote organized a religious community called the Brethren of the Common

Life, which stressed a return to Bible reading, meditation, and the pursuit of holiness. Members adopted a simple, self-supporting lifestyle, living from a common fund, and often earned their livelihood through copying manuscripts. Thomas à Kempis, Desiderius Erasmus, and Martin Luther were influenced by this movement in various degrees.

The Renaissance was a prelude to and preparation for the Reformation. Nothing was more important to the Reformation than the recovery of the biblical languages of Hebrew and Greek. The times were ripe for a re-examination of the teachings and practices of the church in the light of Scripture. At long last, men had solid ground on which to stand as believers and a powerful weapon to employ in combatting the errors and abuses of the church. Faith was no longer understood as unquestioning assent to whatever the church taught, but as knowledge of what God has said in His Word, confidence in its truth and trustworthiness, and submission to its supreme authority for faith and life.

Because many were faithful to what they read in the New Testament, the biblical gospel began to reemerge. Both Huss and Savonarola recognized that after their deaths, the church would experience the much-needed renewal that we call the Reformation. Huss famously predicted that if they burned "this goose" (that is, himself), God would send a swan (which proved to be Luther). Through the Reformation the gospel of the New Testament would be fully rediscovered and preached throughout the world. As we see in these examples in the fifteenth century, it is impossible to hold back the gospel once people rediscover the truth and power of God's Word.

# Luther, Calvin, and the Reformation

The sixteenth century, the beginning of the modern age, is one of the greatest watershed moments in all history, for it witnessed the unfolding of the Protestant Reformation. Benefiting from the biblical scholarship of the Renaissance, the recovery of classical learning, and the zeal of faithful servants in the late fifteenth and early sixteenth centuries, the Reformation was the greatest revival of the Christian church since Pentecost.

Chief among the Reformers was Martin Luther. Born in Northern Germany in 1483, Luther was a bright learner sent by his father to study law at the local university. He was very much the product of medieval spirituality and theology. This theology, with a heavy emphasis on the judgment of God and man's need to achieve salvation from that judgment by doing penance, receiving the sacraments, and doing good works, led him to perpetual doubt regarding his salvation.

One day, Luther was knocked off his horse while traveling and was injured; on another occasion, he was terrified by a thunderstorm. He vowed to become a monk.

As a monk, Luther was troubled by his perceived lack of righteousness despite intense self-discipline and growing knowledge of the Bible. He soon became a Bible lecturer at the local university. He found a troubling text in Romans 1:16–17, about the righteousness of God revealed from heaven. He was terrified of the righteousness of God, seeing it only as God's righteous wrath against sin. But after further study, he came to see that the righteousness Paul had in mind is the righteousness of Jesus Christ that God offers to us as a free gift, to be received by faith. Luther felt the chains of guilt and shame fall away as he grasped this fundamental truth of the gospel for the first time.

In those years, the pope, raising funds to build a new St. Peter's Basilica in Rome, franchised the sale of indulgences or pardons. People could purchase indulgences, which promised deliverance for their deceased loved ones from the rigors of purgatory. In Luther's part of Germany, the commission to sell these pardons went to a Dominican monk, Johan Tetzel, who set about selling them with the zeal of a fishmonger.

Luther, convicted by the immorality of this practice, decided to take action. On October 31, 1517, he nailed his *Ninety-Five Theses* to the castle church door in Wittenberg. These theses, written in Latin, were intended for discussion among scholars and monks in the university. Much of what he wrote was an explanation of the truth of the gospel and a condemnation of the church for failing to believe it and to preach it. Though it was never

Luther's intention, soon the *Ninety-Five Theses* were translated into almost every language in Europe. Like wildfire, the message of justification by faith in Jesus Christ alone spread across the continent. Luther was tried, his teaching was condemned, and he was excommunicated. Concerned friends shielded Luther from danger, however, and he set about the task of translating the Bible into German. In the years that followed, the Reformation took hold in many parts of Europe, and almost always it began with the writings of Luther.

Luther's influence spread and many other Reformers arose to carry on the work. John Calvin of France did the work of ten men in the compass of a relatively short life. At the heart of his life and work was the task of exegeting Scripture, to which he devoted himself day by day. Yet no aspect of life and society went untouched by Calvin's influence. Not only theology, worship, church polity, and missions, but also education, government, economics, industry, and social work all bear the imprint of Calvin's thought. Consequently, some say that Calvin wielded greater influence over our history and culture than any other individual in the last millennium or since the close of the New Testament canon.

Other Reformers included Philip Melanchthon in Germany, Ulrich Zwingli and Heinrich Bullinger in Switzerland, Peter Martyr Vermigli in Italy, John Knox in Scotland, and Thomas Cranmer in England. Much has been written about these individuals and many others who contributed to the Protestant Reformation. Believers today are indebted to their work and testimony. Though not without faults and failures, Christians in the days of the Reformation were bursting with the power and the energy of the gospel. This energy would continue to spread in the years following the Reformation.

# Reforming the Church in England

Reformation came to England during the reign of Henry VIII (r. 1509–1547), but not until the reign of his daughter Elizabeth I (r. 1558–1603) did it gain a firm footing. Elizabeth put England firmly in the Protestant camp, but soon it became clear that Elizabeth wanted a church that was, as Robert Walton writes, "Calvinistic in theology, Erastian in church order and government, and largely mediaeval in liturgy." Those who sought further reformation of the national church were derided as Puritans. Many had lived in Geneva or the Netherlands as refugees during the reign of Queen Mary (r. 1553–1558), and they looked on the churches of those lands as models for England. Elizabeth's *via media* ("middle way") fell far short of their idea of what a Reformed church ought to be.

Initially, Puritan concerns centered on reforming the church's liturgy. They objected to ceremonies such as the signing of the cross in baptism or kneeling to receive the Lord's Supper. Later, as Elizabeth's bishops stood in their way, they began to advocate Presbyterian church polity. More radical elements argued for congregationalism. Some despaired of reforming the Church of England from within and separated from it.

While differing on church polity, the Puritans—who included such notables as William Perkins, Matthew Henry, John Owen, Thomas Goodwin, John Bunyan, John Flavel, and Thomas Watson—were united by a concern to maintain faithful preaching of the gospel and teach sound doctrine; to promote true conversion, personal faith, and practical godliness; and to bring God's Word to bear on all aspects of life, as individuals, in families, and in the nation at large. In short, doctrinally,

Puritanism was a kind of vigorous Calvinism; experientially, it was warm and contagious; evangelistically, it was aggressive, yet tender; ecclesiastically, it was theocentric and worshipful; and politically, it aimed to be scriptural and balanced.

When James VI of Scotland came to the English throne following the death of Elizabeth in 1603, Puritan hopes for a reformed national church were renewed. But as James I of England, he renounced his Presbyterian upbringing in favor of an episcopal establishment that would strengthen his hold on power. He crushed the hopes of the Puritans, though he sanctioned a new translation of the Scriptures—the King James Version, produced in 1611.

Theologically, the Puritans and their opponents had largely agreed on issues relating to soteriology, for nearly all of them were Calvinists. But in the 1620s, when Charles I came to power, he began to appoint Arminians to high positions in the Church of England.

Puritan theologians were unsparing in their criticism of Arminianism. But Archbishop William Laud, preferred by Charles I, sought to promote Arminian theology as well as to enhance the ceremonial aspects of public worship so offensive to the Puritans. Drastic measures were used to secure conformity to the Book of Common Prayer and to silence or punish dissent. Finally, Charles alienated Scottish Presbyterians when he tried to impose a version of the English liturgy on the Church of Scotland. The Presbyterians of Scotland and the Puritans of England united in determination to resist such tyranny. The result was civil war in England and Scotland, pitting forces loyal to the king against the army of Parliament, commanded by Oliver Cromwell, often hailed as the greatest Englishman of his century. Charles lost his throne and his life in 1649. For a time, it seemed that the Puritans had triumphed. The high-water mark of Puritanism was the Westminster Assembly of Divines, which met from 1643 to 1652.

But by 1662, the tide had turned and the monarchy was restored. Under Charles II, new measures were taken to secure conformity and crush dissent. Two thousand Puritan ministers were ejected from their pulpits in the Church of England. The authorities hounded them, suppressed them as ministers, and jailed them as criminals. For decades in Scotland, the crown waged war against the Presbyterians who had covenanted to maintain the Reformed faith, worship, and order of their national church, even to the death.

Though English Puritanism faded by the end of the seventeenth century, its impact on the Scottish Covenanters, the Dutch Further Reformation, New England Puritanism, and German Pietism was profound. That legacy continues today through the remarkable resurgence of Puritan literature that has transpired in the last fifty years—approximately eight hundred reprinted volumes.

# The Great Awakening

By the eighteenth century, Christian Europe had wearied of constant religious strife and bloodshed. Intellectuals embraced the Enlightenment ideal of reason as the ultimate authority. Theology was made subject to philosophy. Deism taught that God created the world, subjected it to natural law, and let nature take its course. This was not the personal God of the Bible; deism was a rejection of revelation in the name of reason. Rationalism prevailed in the eighteenth century and continues to influence theology today.

The Christian pulpit was subverted by the new theology. The gospel ("the power of God unto salvation") was supplanted by a message of thoughtful moderation and good deeds. This powerless substitute had little appeal to the masses. They were left to sink down in unbelief, drunkenness, fornication, gambling, and worse. The church became irrelevant to many people, highborn and low. No one would have guessed that a great revival was at hand.

The revival first appeared in Wales. In the early 1730s, two men who were to lead the revival in Wales—Howell Harris and Daniel Rowland—were converted. By 1750, their preaching and godliness, and that of others, had brought about the creation of 433 religious societies. These societies, whose members called themselves Calvinistic Methodists, set the tone and character of Christianity in Wales for two centuries. All the early Calvinistic Methodist leaders were convinced of the necessity of the Holy Spirit's power and anointing on their ministries.

The year 1735 also saw the conversion of George Whitefield, the leading preacher of the revival on both sides of the Atlantic. In 1732,

Whitefield met John Wesley and his brother Charles, who belonged to a religious society known to history as "the Holy Club." Devout Anglicans, these men set out to pursue holiness by a rigorous discipline or method, and thus were decried as "Methodists." The Wesley brothers also became luminaries of the evangelical revival in England.

German Pietists known as the Moravians deeply influenced John Wesley. The Moravians were led by Nicolaus von Zinzendorf. Influenced by the warm piety of Jacob Spener, Zinzendorf gathered a group of like-minded believers yearning for a more experiential faith than that of the lifeless Lutheranism of eighteenth-century Germany. Their missionary efforts throughout the world in the eighteenth century were renowned.

Wesley was finally converted at a Moravian meeting in Aldersgate Street, London, in 1738. The preface to Martin Luther's commentary on Romans was read aloud, and Wesley felt his heart "strangely warmed" as he listened to Luther's account of the change God works in the heart through faith. Then and there he obtained assurance of salvation and forgiveness of sins. Heralded as "the new birth," this experiential emphasis became the warp and woof of the Great Awakening and the evangelical preaching of Whitefield, Wesley, and others of the era.

Revival also broke out among the sons of the Puritans in New England. Jonathan Edwards wrote an account of the marvelous awakening taking place in his Massachusetts congregation. In the early years of his pastorate in Northampton, his people were outwardly orthodox, but showed few signs of inward religion. In the early 1730s, Edwards observed a growing sensitivity toward sin. In a town of about twelve hundred people, Edwards reckoned that some three hundred were saved in about six months. At the revival's height in 1735, about thirty people a week professed conversion. Soon revival was breaking out in all the colonies. Estimates of those converted in

New England alone, where the population was around a quarter of a million people, ranged from twenty-five thousand to fifty thousand.

This revival also included concentrated mission efforts among the Native Americans. Following in the footsteps of John Eliot, men such as David Brainerd and, later, Edwards himself set out to evangelize the native peoples of the New World. Though these efforts produced mixed results, Brainerd's spiritual diary continues to be an inspiration to missionaries today.

What this fallen world needs is not reason, but the saving grace that transforms people for Christ. The guiding lights of the Great Awakening demonstrated this fact. The evangelistic fervor of the Great Awakening produced a significant missionary expansion that aimed at reaching the whole world for Christ. It also produced a piety focused on conversion and growth in grace through knowing God's Word. We do well to honor and continue that legacy today.

# Beginnings of Modern Theology and Kingdom Builders

Two German philosophers cast a long shadow over the church during the nineteenth century: Immanuel Kant and Friedrich Schleiermacher. Both profoundly influenced modern theology. Kant argued that it is impossible for us to have immediate knowledge of God. Part of his philosophy posited that since all of our knowledge is gained by sense experience, it is not possible for us to have immediate knowledge of anything that lies behind sense experience. We can know the world we live in, but when it comes to that which transcends the physical world, as God does, we can have no knowledge at all. On this basis, Kant rejected both the natural theology of the rationalists and the experiential religion of the pietists.

Schleiermacher was a philosopher who served as a minister in the church. He perceived a general despising of Christianity in Europe, as something out of touch with modern sensibilities. Schleiermacher was concerned with salvaging the Christian faith. *On Religion: Speeches to Its Cultured Despisers* was his response to this perception. Schleiermacher redefined the nature of faith, how one should relate to God, and the person and work of Jesus Christ. He defined religion as the feeling of dependence on God. Jesus, he said, was a model to strive after, and the church was only a community of individuals sharing a common experience. He jettisoned orthodox Christian doctrine for experience.

Though different in their approaches, these men were very similar in their conclusions. They agreed that God is, at best, a product of our experience. Experience trumped revealed truth. Both reason and revelation were divorced from faith, and faith itself was reduced to a feeling. As a result, many today no longer believe in an objective knowledge of God.

The work of God went forward, however, in two great revivals, the Second Great Awakening at the beginning of the century in the United States and the Revival of 1859 on both sides of the Atlantic, not to mention lesser revivals in various places. The church awakened once more to her true calling—to preach the gospel to the ends of the earth. Missionaries went out from many parts of Europe and North America to build God's kingdom in Africa, Asia, and Latin America.

One of these kingdom builders was William Carey. He was a cobbler by trade. God gripped his heart and gave him a vision for evangelizing the world. He went to India in 1793 as a cobbler. Within five years, he had learned Sanskrit and translated the whole Bible into Bengali. By the end of his life, he had supervised translations of the Bible into thirty-six languages and helped launch the great missionary movement of the nineteenth century. Another great missionary from this period was Henry Martyn, who translated the New Testament into Hindustani, Arabic, and Persian, giving his life for the spread of the gospel of Jesus Christ. Others included Robert Moffat, David Livingstone, John Paton, Andrew Gordon, and Hudson Taylor. These were days of great expansion of the British Empire, and in that context, God sent His servants out to the ends of the earth.

The revival of the church and her missionary enterprise was encouraged by the pulpit ministry of gifted preachers such as Charles Spurgeon, whose sermons have been read perhaps by more people than those of any other preacher in church history. Then, too, the gospel fanned out through America and beyond through the influence of Princeton Seminary, under the aegis of devout scholars such as Archibald Alexander, Samuel Miller, and Charles Hodge, who schooled generations of faithful gospel ministers in Reformed truth.

All of these men, and multitudes more, brought God's Word and the knowledge of God in Jesus Christ to the ends of the earth. The contempt of "cultured despisers" takes nothing away from the power and truth of God's Word. God demonstrated His wisdom in that, even as people in Europe began despising the gospel, He was already preparing to go somewhere else. Surely we should pray that God would use us to continue that work of the gospel proclamation in the world today.

# The Age of Paradoxes

The twentieth century was a time of great paradoxes, as the church fell into decline in some parts of the world, but grew and flourished in others. In the first two decades, many in the West envisioned the triumph of Christianity in a golden age of peace and progress for the human race, but this vision died in the carnage and destruction of two world wars.

Rationalistic Modernism assailed the trustworthiness of Holy Scripture, sending great denominations into swift decline, as "the battle for the Bible" beset them. At the same time, Pentecostalism appeared as a tiny offshoot of Methodism and grew into a significant third force in Christendom, augmented by the charismatic movement of the 1970s. The Reformed faith was eclipsed in the early decades of the century, but since 1960, has recovered on both sides of the Atlantic, extending its reach to many parts of the developing world.

As decadent Western churches retreated from missionary work, under pressure of declining memberships and shrinking revenue, the newly planted churches of Africa and Asia grew apace. Communism waged a long and brutal campaign to destroy Christianity in the name of materialism and atheism, but failed, falling into the dustbin of history. There is a vibrant church in Russia today, and more Christians in China than in any other nation in the world. The church in the West has declined in faith and numbers, poisoned by Modernism, battered by secularism, and emasculated by worldliness. But God has continued to send forth His Word to the ends of the earth, bringing people to Himself through Christ, planting churches everywhere, and building His kingdom in the hearts of His redeemed people.

The twentieth century was hard on the churches in Europe and North America. At the beginning of the century, in many places, nearly everyone went to church as a matter of course. The rejection of evangelical theology and biblical Calvinism was regarded as a necessary adjustment to changing times; few could see that it would end with the "Death of God" theology of the 1960s. For a time, the deceptive "Neo-Orthodoxy" of Karl Barth promised to save the church from sterile, destructive Modernism, only to disappoint all but its most zealous exponents. In the wake of the two world wars, thousands gave up churchgoing in Britain, the Netherlands, and elsewhere in Europe. Churchgoing increased in the United States during the 1950s, only to fall off sharply in the 1960s, though it remained considerably higher than in Europe.

There were exceptions to the general rule. Evangelicals belatedly realized that their denominations had been hijacked by Modernism and began to protest in the name of the "fundamentals" of the faith. For better or worse, "Fundamentalism" became a force in American church life. To stem the tide of unbelief, mass evangelistic campaigns were organized in urban centers, led by Billy Sunday and, later, Billy Graham. Movements to recover the historic Reformed faith were led by able men such as J. Gresham Machen, founder of Westminster Seminary and the Orthodox Presbyterian Church. In Britain, D. Martyn Lloyd-Jones drew large congregations to London's Westminster Chapel, and through his influence, the Banner of Truth Trust began to republish outstanding but long-forgotten works of Reformed and Puritan theology.

Meanwhile, the younger churches of the developing Third World, planted by missionaries in the nineteenth century, began to flourish. In Latin America, Pentecostalism succeeded in breaking the iron grip of Roman Catholicism and drew many thousands into its ranks. Presbyterian and Reformed churches were planted in the Caribbean islands, as well as in Central and South America. In Asia, there came to be Christians of many kinds in China, a thriving if sometimes-discordant family of Presbyterian churches in Korea, and significant numbers of Reformed churches in India, Pakistan, Sri Lanka, and elsewhere. As for Africa, huge numbers of Christians adhered to churches of all kinds, often coming into conflict with the forces of Islam spreading down from the north.

In the Middle East, historic Christian populations are shrinking under persecution at the hands of militant Islamists. The clash with Islam continues in Pakistan, Indonesia, and elsewhere in the world. But the record of church history teaches us to hold fast to Christ, assured that He is with us always, even to the end of the world. He will build up His church and kingdom to all generations.